NATIVE PEOPLES

by William McCay

Table of Contents

CHAPTER 1

What Are Native Peoples?

History often tells about people coming to live in a new land. For example, people from many countries have come to America. But there are groups of people who have lived in the same place for thousands of years.

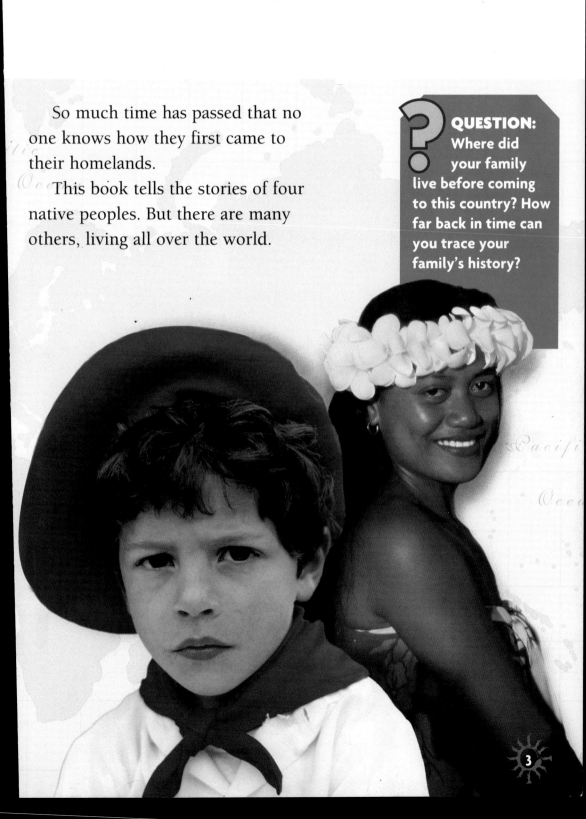

So much time has passed that no one knows how they first came to their homelands.

This book tells the stories of four native peoples. But there are many others, living all over the world.

? **QUESTION:** Where did your family live before coming to this country? How far back in time can you trace your family's history?

3

The Inuit

The Inuit (IH-noo-wit) people live in the far north in parts of Asia, Europe, and North America. Most Inuit land is north of the **Arctic Circle.**

Many people call the Inuit **"Eskimos,"** but that is actually a name given to them by certain Native American tribes. The word "Eskimo" means "men who eat raw meat." In the Inuits' own language, "Inuit" means "the people."

The Inuit came to North America from Asia. The part of North America that is now Alaska is separated from Asia by a narrow strip of water called the Bering Strait.

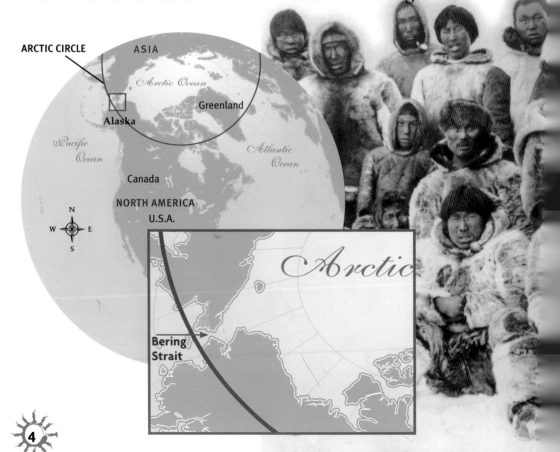

ARCTIC CIRCLE
ASIA
Arctic Ocean
Greenland
Alaska
Pacific Ocean
Atlantic Ocean
Canada
NORTH AMERICA
U.S.A.
N
W   E
S

Arctic

Bering Strait

Thousands of years ago, there was land where the Bering Strait is now. The Inuits' ancestors probably crossed over this land into what is now Alaska. By the year 1200 A.D., the Inuit had traveled all the way to Greenland.

↑ Inuit tools were often made of wood, stone, or bone.

←This group of Inuit was photographed in 1914.

Depending on the time of year, different animals would walk, fly, or swim through Inuit territory.

Most Inuit lived in a world of rock, ice, and tundra—land where the soil always stays frozen. They couldn't grow food. Instead, they hunted. Much of what they ate was meat. And much of that meat wasn't cooked.

Depending on the time of year, different animals would walk, fly, or swim through Inuit territory. The Inuit followed these animals to get the food they needed. They also fished in rivers, lakes, and bays.

During the summer hunting season, Inuit often lived in tents made of **caribou** hide. In winter, some Inuit went out on the thick ice sheets that formed on the sea. Hunters stood for hours in freezing weather beside holes in the ice. Seals would come to these holes to breathe. Then the hunters would throw special spears called **harpoons** to kill the seals for the

⬆ This painting from 1879 shows an American expedition at an Inuit village. The midnight sun is in the sky, even though it is nighttime. The houses are made of caribou skin.

meat that they needed to eat during the winter.

These hunters built homes out of snow. They cut blocks of packed snow and set them in a circle. The houses were dome-shaped. Oil-burning lamps or small fires gave light and warmth. In Inuit, the word **"igloo"** just means "house."

↑ Meat from one white whale could feed a family all winter. The Inuit made sleds out of whalebone, and they burned oil, made from whale fat, to get light and heat.

↑ Inuit hunted the caribou—a kind of deer—for more than just meat. They used the antlers to make tools, the skin to make beds and tents, and the guts to make thread and rope.

↑ Sealskin was used for clothing and making boats.

To live through the harsh arctic winters, the Inuit learned to dress in several layers of clothing to stay warm.

Once, only travelers to the far north saw the work of Inuit artists. Nowadays, many people can appreciate Inuit carved figures in wood, ivory, and soapstone.

The Inuit gave the world the **kayak**, a special kind of canoe. The whole boat is covered in sealskin, with a hole just large enough for a person to get in.

To live through the harsh arctic winters, the Inuit learned to dress in several layers of clothing to stay warm. They also invented the **parka**. This hooded coat is loose enough to be comfortable, but tight at the wrists and the neck to keep the wearer warm. The Inuit sewed these parkas out of animal skins with the furry side in for warmth.

Inuit parka →

Inuit ↓
carving

Some Inuit still follow the ancient ways. But contact with other cultures has changed the Inuit way of life. People came in ships to hunt the whales the Inuit needed for meat and oil. The Inuit began trading furs for tools and rifles. To get the furs, they had to hunt and kill many more animals—animals that could have been used for food.

Today, many Inuit live in homes close to trading posts or near towns where they can find

Inuit kayak ↑

work. They can't live in the old way. But often, they have trouble finding good jobs.

The Inuit live under governments of many nations, but they are gaining the right to rule themselves. The people of the north are working together. They have formed an organization called the Inuit Circumpolar Conference, which brings Inuit people from different countries together.

↑ **This Inuit man is using a bow similar to the ones that the ancient Inuit used.**

9

The Tuareg

T he Tuareg (TWAH-reg) are an African people. They live in **desert** and semi-arid areas in the northwestern part of the continent.

Scientists who study ancient peoples believe that the Tuareg have lived in North Africa for a very long time—more than 4,000 years. During their long history, the lands where the Tuareg live have been invaded and conquered by different people. But the Tuareg have always

The Sahara is larger than the entire United States. The Tuareg wander over more than half of this area.
↓

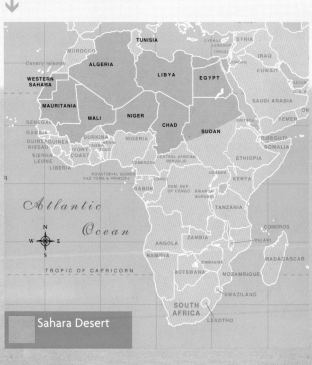

Sahara Desert

fought fiercely for their independence and the right to live in their traditional ways. For example, about 1,200 years ago, Arabs conquered North Africa. The Tuareg fought the Arab invaders, although they finally accepted their **Muslim** religion. They fought just as stubbornly when the French came to North Africa in the 1800s.

◆◆

Tuareg society is controlled by nobles, the most important and powerful people.

Most Tuareg are **nomads** who wander from place to place instead of settling down in permanent homes. These people are always moving their herds of cattle, goats, and camels to new grazing lands and from one watering hole to the next.

Tuareg society is controlled by nobles, the most important and powerful people. Second in importance are the warriors. Then come the craftspeople who make weapons and tools.

At the bottom are farmers, who must stay on their land and are not free to wander. Once the least important people were the slaves, but there are no slaves among the Tuareg now.

↑ **Tuareg men wear veils to protect themselves from sun and sand. The Tuareg are called "the blue people" because the blue dye from their clothes stains their bodies.**

↑ **Tuareg dagger**

The Tuareg make beautiful things. They are famous for the objects they make out of leather—especially saddles. They also make excellent swords. The Tuareg believe that their craftspeople have magical powers.

↑ **A Tuareg man rides on his camel with a handcrafted saddle.**

People all over the world buy Tuareg jewelry. But here is an interesting fact. The Tuareg call gold an "impure" metal. They place a higher value on silver and make most of their jewelry out of silver.

← **Women are very important among the Tuareg. They do not wear veils, as most Muslim women do. Everything children inherit, even their importance in the tribe, comes from their mothers rather than their fathers.**

↑ **The age-old customs of Tuareg life may soon pass away.**

In recent times, the Tuareg's worst problem has been the weather. For many years, the area where the Tuareg live suffered a **drought**, a time when no rain falls. Lack of water killed the farmers' crops. The nomads' animal herds died of thirst. People starved to death. Now all the Tuareg—from nobles to farmers—are poor.

Many Tuareg now stay around the towns and cities at the edge of the Sahara. The young men think that getting a job and settling down is easier than life in the desert. Soon, these proud desert warriors may be just a memory.

The Polynesians

The Polynesians are native peoples of Polynesia, a group of islands located in the Pacific Ocean. The ancestors of the Polynesians probably lived in China and Southeast Asia. They lived on the seacoast and fished. Using their fishing boats, they traveled down the Malay peninsula. Then they spread across the islands of Indonesia. About 3,500 years ago, these people reached the islands of Fiji and Samoa. From there, they spread across the Pacific.

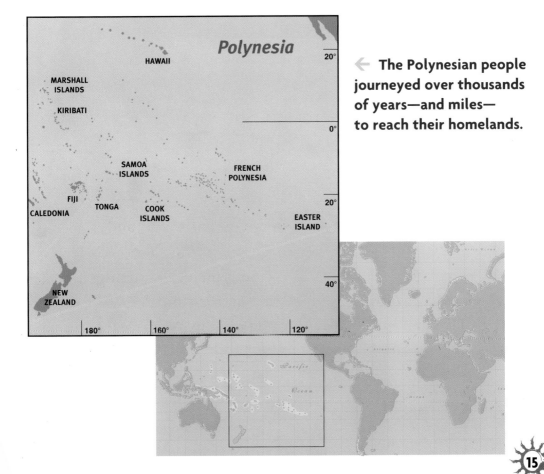

← The Polynesian people journeyed over thousands of years—and miles— to reach their homelands.

The Polynesians made canoes and built houses using trees and other plants that were available.

The Polynesians sailed in large canoes, each carved from a single tree. A deck connected two canoes together to make a

In double canoes like these, the Polynesians traveled great distances to new homes.

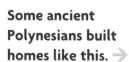

Some ancient Polynesians built homes like this. →

double canoe, and a single mast held a sail. These boats were large enough to carry the people and their animals, such as chickens and pigs.

When they reached their destination, the Polynesians needed food, clothing, and shelter. From the sea, they got fish and shellfish to eat. They made cloth from the bark of trees. They made canoes and built houses using trees and other available plants.

How much land can you use for growing food? How many trees can you cut down for wood to build houses, canoes, and tools?

IT'S A Fact

The Polynesian word spelled "tabu," "tapu," or "tampu" means "set aside." It referred to the fact that important resources needed to be preserved. It has come into English as "taboo," which means something that is strictly forbidden.

But living on an island, even a large one, presents special problems. The natural resources are very limited. Is there enough fresh water for drinking and growing crops? How much land can you use for growing food? How many trees can you cut down for wood to build houses, canoes, and tools?

Polynesians found a way to keep these things from being used up. They developed "**taboos**," or strict rules against wasting or destroying important resources such as water, land, and trees. People who didn't obey the taboos were threatening the lives of others.

↑ **A stream runs beside a road in the town of Avarua, on the island of Rarotonga, in the Cook Islands.**

THE FALL OF EASTER ISLAND

Hundreds of years ago, Easter Island was a lush tropical paradise. However, the people who settled there did not follow strict rules against using up the natural resources. They cut down all of the trees to make boats, homes, and tools for moving their huge stone statues. The topsoil eroded. Their crops failed. Food became very scarce. They could not even build canoes to leave the island. Many thousands of people died of starvation.

The strangers from Europe and America brought diseases that had never been known before on the islands.

↑ **Captain James Cook**

The Polynesians' lives changed abruptly when European explorers sailed to the islands from the 1500s through the 1700s.

The most famous of these explorers was the Englishman Captain James Cook of the British Royal Navy, who explored many islands in the Pacific Ocean.

Large, powerful countries did not just explore the countries they found. They took them over and ruled them. The Polynesian islands were no exception. Britain took control of New Zealand and Tonga. The French got Tahiti and other islands. Hawaii was taken over by the United States. The newcomers took the best land for themselves.

TONGA

NEW ZEALAND

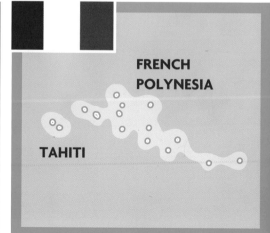

FRENCH POLYNESIA

TAHITI

They set up plantations to grow bananas, pineapples, and sugar cane. Loggers came in to cut down trees.

The strangers from Europe and America brought diseases that had never been known before on the islands. Thousands of Polynesians died of measles, smallpox, flu, and tuberculosis.

By the 1880s, many people thought the Polynesian people would all die off. But they were wrong. There are many thousands of Polynesian people living today on islands in the South Pacific—in New Zealand to the south, Hawaii to the north, and Easter Island to the east.

IT'S A
Fact

Hawaii had a Polynesian royal family until the last queen, Liliukalani, was overthrown in 1893. After that, the Hawaiian islands were governed by the United States.

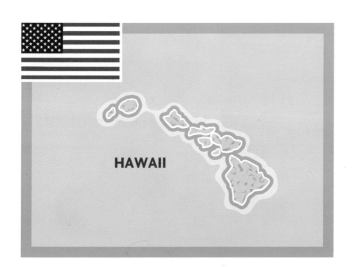

HAWAII

Kava is an herb grown on the Polynesian islands that was used originally to make a sacred drink. Today, people buy Kava tablets in stores. They use the herb to help them sleep and to fight headaches.

The Polynesian culture has had an important influence on the rest of the world. The geometric patterns of their clothing are imitated on shirts all over the world. Hawaiian music and Polynesian dancing are popular with many people.

Kava is an herb grown on the Polynesian islands that was used originally to make a sacred drink. Today, people buy Kava tablets in stores. They use the herb to help them sleep and to fight headaches.

This photograph was taken in Tahiti around 1880. It shows a young Tahitian man wearing a Polynesian print cloth. ↓

Although all the islands share a cultural tradition, their forms of governments differ. For example, Tonga, Western Samoa, and Fiji are independent. Other Polynesian islands are controlled by other countries. Tahiti has a French governor, and Easter Island is ruled by Chile. In New Zealand and Hawaii, the native Polynesian people are **minorities** in their old homelands. However, the Polynesian people are struggling to maintain their cultural traditions and identity.

IT'S A Fact

Years ago, an American dentist visiting Polynesia noticed that the islanders had very healthy teeth. He learned that one of their foods, taro root, is rich in **fluoride**. He went home and developed fluoride toothpaste.

← Tongan father and his children

The Basques

In Europe, the Pyrenees (PEER-eh-neez) mountains mark the border between present day France and Spain. Long before either France or Spain existed, the Basque (BASK) people lived in this area. In Spanish, the Basques are called "Vascon." "Basque" is their French name. But in their own language, they call themselves "Euskaldunak" (yoo-SKAL-duh-nak). That means "one who speaks our language."

The first mention of the Basques comes from ancient Roman writings from more than 2,000 years ago. But modern science can trace the Basques back 40,000 years!

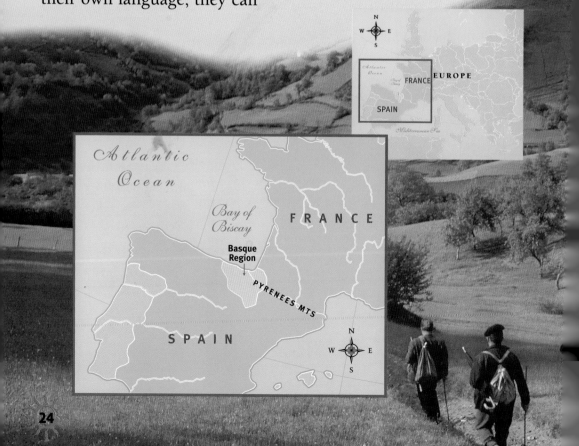

Scientists think that the Basques are descended from the **Cro-Magnon**—Stone Age people who lived in caves about 40,000 years ago. Since then, whole peoples and nations have appeared and disappeared. But the Basques have survived and held onto their rugged homeland.

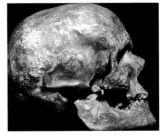

↑ Scientists believe that the people who left these 40,000-year-old bones still have distant relatives living today—the Basques.

← The area where the Basques live is farm country like this.

For a long time, the Basques were independent even though their lands were invaded by many people, such as the Romans, the Moors from North Africa, and later, the French and Spanish.

Today **fueros** (foo-ER-oze), the local governing assemblies, meet in buildings whose history goes back hundreds of years. This is the Plaza de los Fueros, in Tudela, Spain. ↓

Traditionally, the Basques prefer to live on small farms rather than in big cities. A farmer's oldest son inherits all the land. Younger sons must go off and search for jobs.

Many Basques go to sea as fishermen or sailors. Others take care of animals. Some Basques have come to America to herd sheep.

The Basques have had a long, violent history. For a long time, the Basques were independent even though their lands were invaded by many people, such as the Romans, the Moors from North Africa, and later, the French and Spanish. Basques ruled themselves, making laws through their local councils, called fueros.

Basque farmer herding sheep →

IT'S A Fact

Basques gave the world the sport of jai-alai (HY-ly). It's a fast-moving handball game played with special hand scoops. The name "jai-alai" comes from the Basque words for "merry festival."

Picasso created a painting that has become a universal symbol of the horrors of war.

The last war that the Basques fought in was the Spanish **Civil War**, in 1937. In this war, one part of Spain was fighting another part of the same country. The Basques were fighting on one side, and the Germans were helping the other side.

German warplanes bombed the Basque village of Guernica (gair-NEE-kuh). Most of the town was burned or destroyed. Many people were killed. When the Spanish artist Pablo Picasso heard about the destruction, he was shocked. He created a painting that has become a universal symbol of the horrors of war.

The Basques' enemies won the civil war. The victors treated the Basques harshly, making it illegal to speak the Basque language! Eventually, a new government came to power and gave the Basques the right

↑ Pablo Picasso's *Guernica* is considered one of the great works of modern art.

to make some of their own rules. Still, many Basques want to set up an independent Basque nation.

No one can say what the future holds, but one thing is certain. The Basques have kept their language and their way of life for thousands of years. Even the Basques who have gone to other lands are proud to be Euskaldunak.

⬇ **Basque farmers still farm their land the way their ancestors have done for thousands of years.**

Native Peoples of the World

You have met four native peoples of the world, but there are many more. Here is a list of some other native peoples and where they live. You may want to find out more about them. Just remember, for every group on this list, there are hundreds more.

Some native peoples of the world

Aborigines (a-buh-RIH-jih-neez)	Australia
Ainu (I-noo)	northern Japan
Bushmen	Kalahari Desert, Africa
Hmong (MUNG)	Vietnam
Lapps	Scandinavia
Miskito (mis-KEE-toh)	Central America
Indians	Nicaragua
Native American tribes	North America
Yanomami Indians (yah-noh-MAH-mee)	Amazon rain forest, South America

Glossary

Arctic Circle (ARK-tik SER-kul) an imaginary circle around Earth at a about 66 degrees north latitude

caribou (KAIR-ih-boo) a deerlike animal living in the far northern part of North America; a reindeer

civil war (SIH-vul WOR) war between groups or areas in the same country

Cro-Magnon (kroh-MAG-nun) prehistoric people who lived in Europe 40,000 years ago

desert (DEH-zert) a very dry area where it rarely rains

drought (DROWT) a dry period when rain doesn't fall for a long time

Eskimo (ES-kih-moh) a name given by Native Americans to the Inuit, meaning "men who eat raw meat"

fluoride (FLOR-ide) a chemical that helps prevent cavities in teeth

fuero (foo-ER-oh) Basque local self-governing council

harpoon (har-POON) a special sort of spear with a rope attached for hunting sea animals

igloo (IH-gloo) dome-shaped house made of snow by the Inuit people

jai-alai (HY-ly) fast-moving game in which players use scoop-shaped baskets strapped to their wrists to fling a ball against a wall

kava (KAH-vuh) a pepper plant whose roots are used to make a special Polynesian drink

kayak (KY-ak) an Inuit canoe; animal skins cover its whole wooden frame except for a hole fitting the waist of the paddler

minority (mih-NOR-ih-tee) a group of people who make up only a fraction of a larger group

Muslim (MUZ-lim) a religion based on the teachings of Muhammad

nomads (NOH-madz) people with no permanent homes who wander in search of food or water

parka (PAR-kuh) a hooded coat invented by the Inuit

taboo (TA-boo) something that is forbidden; the rules set up by Polynesians to protect scarce resources

Index